UNDERCOVER STORY

THE HIDDEN STORY OF

EATING
DISORDERS

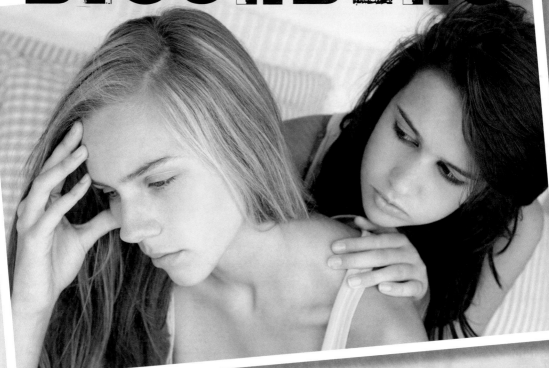

Sarah Levete

rosen publishing's
rosen central

New York

Published in 2014 by The Rosen Publishing Group, Inc.
29 East 21st Street
New York, NY 10010

First Edition   FEB 1 7 2015

Produced for Rosen by Calcium Creative Ltd.
Editors for Calcium Creative Ltd.: Sarah Eason and Ronne Randall
Designer: Keith Williams

Photo credits: Cover: Dreamstime: Lisavan. Inside: Dreamstime: Anpet2000 28, Barsik 31, Bjwynnyk 16, Bobsphotography 38, Featureflash 43, Grafvision 34, Hjalmeida 25, Kurniawan1972 41, Monkeybusinessimages 1, 27, 32, 36, Phakimata 44; Shutterstock: Featureflash 19, Maga 4, Monkey Business Images 10, 14, 15, 22, Bombaert Patrick 5, Ana Blazic Pavlovic 6, 20, Sidarta 17, Simone van den Berg 12, Angela Waye 8, Ivonne Wierink 22, MILA Zed 7.

Library of Congress Cataloging-in-Publication Data

Levete, Sarah.
The hidden story of eating disorders/Sarah Levete.—First edition.
     pages cm.—(Undercover story)
Audience: Grades 5-8.
Includes bibliographical references and index.
ISBN 978-1-4777-2795-9 (library binding)
1. Eating disorders—Juvenile literature. I. Title.
RC552.E18L485 2014
616.85'26—dc23

                                                                2013021951

Manufactured in the United States of America

CPSIA Compliance Information: #W14YA: For further information, contact Rosen Publishing, New York, New York, at 1-800-237-9932.

CONTENTS

INTRODUCTION The Truth About Eating Disorders   4

CHAPTER ONE Dying to Eat   6

CHAPTER TWO Living With an Eating Disorder   14

CHAPTER THREE Who Suffers and Why?   24

CHAPTER FOUR Getting Help   32

CHAPTER FIVE The Importance of Well-Being   38

EATING DISORDERS—THE TRUTH   44

GLOSSARY   46

FOR MORE INFORMATION   47

INDEX   48

THE TRUTH ABOUT EATING DISORDERS

Everyone needs to eat—food is fuel and nourishment for the body. Most people have favorite foods they enjoy, or foods that they don't like. Eating with friends and family can be a sociable and enjoyable time. Everyone's eating patterns are different and can vary according to changes in routine. For instance, someone may eat more sugary snacks on vacation but cut them out when they get home—and it's not a big deal. However, for some people, eating is neither about nutrition nor enjoyment—food has become a way of coping with other difficult feelings.

A DIFFICULT ILLNESS

Eating disorders are complex illnesses. They can seriously harm physical health and mental well-being. Someone with an eating disorder is obsessed with what he or she can and can't eat, weight, and body image.

It's possible for anyone to develop an eating disorder, but no one can catch one—they are not infectious diseases. Eating disorders often start as diets, but the diet becomes out of control. The individual no longer has a healthy or rational attitude to food and eating.

People who suffer from eating disorders fear eating food—they believe even tiny amounts of food will make them gain weight.

BREAKING NEWS

>> According to the National Eating Disorders Association (NEDA), 20 million women and 10 million men in the United States will suffer from some type of eating disorder during their lives.

People can recover from an eating disorder, if they receive the treatment and support they need. It's important to recognize the warning signs of eating disorders, because they can be prevented and early diagnosis helps recovery.

Teenagers are most likely to develop eating disorders, but children as young as six can also suffer.

This book examines what it means to have an eating disorder, why people develop them, and what can be done to support recovery.

>> Eating disorders used to be considered just a female illness. However, research shows that more than 10 percent of patients seen by mental health specialists in eating disorders are male.

CHAPTER ONE

DYING TO EAT

People with anorexia may check their weight several times a day, because they are terrified of getting fat.

Even in the middle of summer, 14-year-old Kitty was shivering. Her hair was falling out in clumps and her breath had a sour smell. Her mother had noticed that Kitty was too thin. Kitty's parents took her to see a doctor and she was diagnosed with the eating disorder anorexia nervosa. Kitty weighed just 71 pounds (32 kg) and was 4 feet, 11 inches (1.2 m) tall. However, she did not feel thin at all.

AN OBSESSION WITH FOOD

Kitty was obsessed with meals. She needed to know in advance what was for dinner each night of the week. Exercise was also very important. Kitty spent hours every night doing sit-ups and push-ups in her room.

BREAKING NEWS

>> More and more children are being hospitalized for eating disorders each year, having starved their bodies to a point where they require serious medical care and attention.

Then Kitty started making excuses to not eat at all. She said she had a stomachache or wasn't hungry. She said she would eat later or that she had already eaten at a friend's house. One hot day that summer, Kitty felt strange and said, "My heart feels funny." She was admitted to the hospital. Her heart was weak and she was dehydrated. The doctors told her that she had to start eating again to get better. But eating is never simple for an anorexic person. It can be the most agonizing thing he or she can imagine doing.

Kitty is just one of millions of people who have an eating disorder. The three main disorders are anorexia, bulimia, and binge eating. Some people also suffer from a combination of eating disorders.

Eating disorders affect boys and men as well as girls and women.

7

People with anorexia nervosa (usually called just anorexia) drastically restrict their food intake in order to lose weight and weigh as little as possible. When people with anorexia look at themselves in the mirror they do not see an accurate reflection.

People with anorexia think they look fat, even if they are shockingly underweight. Anorexia is a serious mental illness that can drastically harm the health of people who suffer from the condition. In severe cases, anorexia can even kill.

Anorexia is not about being on a diet to look slim. Sufferers are dangerously underweight.

OUT OF CONTROL

Anorexia often develops from a diet that becomes out of control. One day of cutting back on meals and watching calorie intake in order to lose weight is not anorexia. However, denying the body essential food over a few weeks can turn into anorexia. When this happens, the diet is no longer about losing a few pounds but has become an intense fear of becoming fat. The illness takes hold and the sufferer becomes obsessed with restricting his or her diet and losing even more weight.

People who suffer from anorexia are terrified of food and often figure out the calories in every mouthful they eat. Sufferers sometimes chew food and then spit it out, unable to bear the thought of extra calories they think will add to their weight. They may even reject a sip of water, believing even this will add to their weight. People with anorexia pretend to eat or say they have already eaten. Sufferers wear baggy clothes to hide their skeletal frame so no one can see how thin they have become.

HITTING THE HEADLINES

DEADLY DISEASE

In 2006, aged 26 years old, Uruguayan model Luisel Ramos died from heart failure. She had reportedly been fasting and starving for weeks, surviving on sugar-free soda drinks and lettuce. Successful model Ana Carolina Reston was told she was too fat when she started modeling. In 2006, she died in the hospital, aged just 21, after living on a diet of tomatoes and apples. Her death was recorded as complications arising from anorexia.

A person suffering from the eating disorder bulimia nervosa (usually known as bulimia) often appears to be a healthy, regular weight. To outsiders he or she appears to be healthy, and as a result his or her eating disorder may continue, in secret, for a long time before family or friends become aware of it. Bulimics have an agonizing relationship with food. They binge on large amounts of food and then get rid of it by making themselves sick or taking laxatives to go to the bathroom. This process of ridding the body of food is called purging.

People who suffer from bulimia may seem to eat normally with their family and friends, but then they secretly purge their body.

BREAKING NEWS

>> A 2009 study by the Healthcare Cost and Utilization Project found that between 1999 and 2006, the number of kids 12 and under admitted to a hospital for eating disorders increased by an enormous 119 percent.

CAUSES OF BULIMIA

As with other eating disorders, there are many reasons why a person becomes bulimic. The illness often starts as a diet. However, when the person breaks the diet or doesn't lose weight, he or she feels miserable and binges on large amounts of food—and then tries to get rid of it by being sick or going to the bathroom. Bulimics frequently binge on cake, candy, or fatty foods—the very foods they want to cut out of their diet. The cycle of bingeing and purging can happen many times in one day. Bulimics often feel intense shame and self-loathing because of their eating disorder. Despite these emotions of self-loathing and remorse, sufferers also feel powerless to stop their destructive cycle of behavior.

UNDERCOVER STORY
THE HIDDEN ILLNESS

Bulimia is more common than anorexia, but it's harder to spot because sufferers are often of average weight and seem to eat regular meals with family or friends. Bulimia is often a hidden illness because sufferers feel so ashamed of their problem and don't want anyone else to know about it. The secrecy and shame can make a sufferer feel even more lonely and unhappy. They turn to food as comfort and then the cycle of bingeing and purging continues.

Lots of people occasionally eat too many cookies or candy, or have an extra portion of food, and it does little harm. However, some people regularly binge and are unable to control the urge to eat large quantities of food. They then eat without feeling hunger or feeling full. They gain weight, and that in turn makes them feel unhappy.

They then eat more to blot out their unhappiness. Compulsive eaters eat for comfort and to escape painful feelings that are difficult to face. They constantly pick at food and feel unable to stop. Binge and compulsive eaters do not eat because of physical hunger. Food becomes a coping mechanism to deal with other problems.

Not everyone with an eating disorder will have the exact same symptoms or share the same behavior around food.

BREAKING NEWS

>> According to NEDA, girls who diet frequently are 12 times as likely to binge than girls who do not diet.

UNDERCOVER STORY

EDNOS

There are often variations in the signs and symptoms of a particular eating disorder, and not everyone will have the same behavior around food. Many people suffer from EDNOS (short for Eating Disorders Not Otherwise Specified). EDNOS are eating disorders that share some, but not all, of the symptoms of bulimia or anorexia.

SECRET EATING

People who suffer from binge eating or compulsive eating disorders often eat alone because they are embarrassed about their behavior. They withdraw from regular socializing because they feel guilty and ashamed about their eating. This isolation makes them turn to food for comfort even more.

Sufferers of these eating disorders often feel empty and inadequate.

Eating makes them feel safe and comforted, but when they are unable to stop bingeing or eating, they feel greater unhappiness with themselves. This leads to more bingeing and overeating.

People who binge or eat compulsively become overweight. Being very overweight can lead to heart problems and movement problems, and puts a person at a higher risk of developing diabetes.

CHAPTER TWO

LIVING WITH AN EATING DISORDER

Leroy's mother was in despair. Her once lively and outgoing son had become withdrawn and moody, shutting his bedroom door as soon as he came home from school. He kept going to the bathroom, coming out looking pale and puffy. He complained of swollen glands and feeling tired. Leroy's parents tried to talk to him, but he shut them out, saying nothing was wrong. His mother took him to the pediatrician, but she could find no medical cause for his symptoms. Friends came over and asked Leroy to play basketball, but he would never go. He refused to go swimming, even during hot, sunny vacations. Leroy's mom put it down to starting a new school and the recent breakup of her marriage.

Eating disorders can make people feel very lonely and hopeless.

BREAKING NEWS

>> Research from NEDA shows that suicide rates are particularly high among people suffering from eating disorders.

Parents are often desperate to get their children to eat normally and to help them find a way out of their suffering.

NOWHERE TO HIDE

When Leroy started to vomit blood and experience terrible stomach cramps, he knew that he could no longer hide his problem. He broke down and, through his tears, told his mother that for months he had been bingeing and making himself sick, sometimes as much as seven times a day. Leroy's mother was relieved finally to know what was wrong with her son. However, she felt guilty that she had not realized what had been happening to him.

Like many people suffering from bulimia, Leroy had felt so ashamed of his condition that he refused to admit he had an eating disorder. He was caught in a terrible cycle, desperate to break the pattern of his behavior but unable to do so.

Bulimia and other eating disorders have a severe effect on both physical and mental well-being. Research shows that more people die from eating disorders than any other type of mental illness.

People with anorexia are so underweight and have lost so much body fat that their bodies desperately try to retain warmth by growing a covering of downy hair over the body and face. However, as the eating disorder worsens, the hair of an anorexic begins to thin and fall out and their skin looks dry and flaky.

Anorexia can make the sufferer feel very cold and tired, but the long-term physical effects are much more serious.

It's common for sufferers to feel faint and weak because they do not eat enough food to give them energy. They feel cold even on a warm day. Without key nutrients, the heart muscle is starved and begins to shrink. The body slows down. This can be extremely dangerous. As the heart slows down and blood pressure drops, heart failure is possible.

BREAKING NEWS

>> Statistics from the Renfrew Centre Foundation for Eating Disorders show that 20 percent of anorexics die early from complications related to their eating disorder, including suicide and heart problems.

THE FUTURE

The long-term effects of anorexia are serious. Being very underweight affects hormones that are responsible for a girl's periods, so young anorexic girls may not start their periods at all. Older girls' periods may stop for a long time. This can lead to difficulties conceiving children when they are adults.

Many people with anorexia also suffer from a bone disease called osteoporosis because they do not have enough calcium in their bodies to keep their bones healthy and strong. Calcium is found in many dairy products such as cheese and milk. Without calcium, bones become weak and break easily, and even a simple fall can result in a broken or shattered bone.

Eating disorders often mask unhappiness that a sufferer is trying to blot out. Actually, the negative relationship with food causes even more emotional distress.

ADDITIONAL PHYSICAL EFFECTS

When a person vomits, acid from the stomach wears away at the protective layer of enamel that covers the teeth. As a result, people with bulimia often have discolored and rotting teeth. The acid produced by the stomach also causes a sore, burning throat, but more seriously it can damage an organ at the back of the throat called the esophagus. Through repeated vomiting, the esophagus can become inflamed and infected. If the esophagus tears and blood appears in a person's vomit, it can be life-threatening.

Overuse of laxatives can lead to constant constipation or diarrhea and stomach pains. There is also a risk of a person becoming addicted to laxatives. If this happens, a person is unable to go to the bathroom normally, and may have embarrassing accidents.

Regular vomiting upsets the body's natural chemical balances and causes dehydration. This causes dizziness, and can lead to irregular heartbeats and even heart failure. People with bulimia often feel tired as a result of dehydration, and their faces look puffy. Blood vessels in the eyes sometimes burst from the pressure of repeated vomiting. Sufferers may have sores and blisters on their hands, which are caused by acid in their vomit irritating and burning the skin on the hands. People may also have pressure marks from their teeth on their hands, created when they make themselves sick.

People with bulimia, like those with anorexia, often lack essential nutrients. In the teenage years when the young body is developing, a lack of vital nutrients can stunt the body's growth and development. In particular, laxatives and vomiting get rid of a very important mineral, potassium. This crucial nutrient is essential for a healthy heart.

Opposite: Even celebrities who appear very confident may be hiding their unhappiness and low self-esteem. Bulimia can affect anyone, whatever his or her lifestyle.

HITTING THE HEADLINES

CELEBRITY SUFFERER

Glamorous singer and celebrity Nicole Scherzinger suffered from bulimia when she was in the girl band the Pussycat Dolls. Quoted on VH1's *Behind the Music*, Nicole revealed that she had fought a decade-long battle with bulimia: "I just hated myself… I hated myself. I really was so disgusted with myself and so embarrassed. I felt so alone. I was in a group, and I never felt so alone in my life… My bulimia was my addiction; hurting myself was my addiction."

People with eating disorders feel ashamed and hate themselves for what they are doing. They know their eating pattern is not making them happy but feel unable stop. The eating disorder becomes a punishment for their behavior.

Even though sufferers' eating may be out of control with bingeing and purging, people with eating disorders often feel this is one area of their lives over which they have control and that makes them feel safe. Food is used as a way of coping with feelings and concerns that the sufferers may not be able to express to other people or even face up to. Sufferers are also often trying to cope with depression or other anxiety problems.

People with eating disorders are tormented by their desperation to break free from the cycle of their eating pattern and their inability to do so.

GOING PUBLIC

In recent years, several high-profile celebrities such as Elton John and Lady Gaga have admitted to suffering from eating disorders including bulimia, in the hope that it will help other people feel brave enough to own up to their problem and seek help. However, it's important not to think that bulimia can't be all that bad because celebrities seem to have such glamorous and charmed lives. It's important to remember how desperate and worthless any eating disorder makes a person feel, even if they look good and lead a high-profile celebrity life.

UNDERCOVER STORY

HIDDEN ILLNESSES

Eating disorders are often hidden because sufferers go to huge lengths to keep their illness secret. Anorexia is easier to diagnose than other eating disorders because a sufferer is very underweight. However, bulimia and other eating disorders are no less dangerous or psychologically damaging than anorexia. Admitting to having an eating disorder or helping someone seek support is very important because research suggests that the earlier a person seeks support, the more likely he or she is to recover.

>> A *People* magazine telephone poll reported that 80 percent of females surveyed said that women in movies and television programs made them feel insecure about their bodies.

Eating disorders put huge pressures on friends and family, who often feel helpless and desperate when they see a loved one battling unhappiness and a troubled relationship with food.

Sufferers often try to hide their illness, pretending to be allergic to certain foods or making an excuse about having eaten earlier.

People with anorexia go to extreme lengths to hide their food, secreting it under the table, in bags, or inside their clothes. Those with bulimia and binge eaters may hide and stash food, and then eat it secretly. Although family and friends may not notice the hidden food, the reality is that they do notice a loved one becoming withdrawn, unhappy, and isolated.

Sufferers often avoid social situations because they are so terrified of eating in public or of missing what they consider crucial exercise.

COPING WITH EATING

Most young people enjoy chatting with friends, arranging to meet for a milk shake or to go and hang out in the park. These social arrangements may involve food, such as eating out or going over to a friend's house for a meal. For most people, this type of activity is a fun part of everyday life. However, for people with eating disorders, this regular activity is filled with terror. How will they avoid food? Will they eat too much?

How can they fit in extra exercise to get rid of the weight they will have gained from eating just one carrot? Will anyone notice them pretending to eat? These are just some of the thoughts likely to run through the mind of a person suffering from an eating disorder when faced with a social activity. People who suffer from eating disorders are continually tormented by thoughts of food and eating or not eating.

UNDERCOVER STORY
EXERCISE EXCESS

It's healthy to exercise and keep fit, but people with eating disorders often exercise to extreme lengths in order to burn off any calories they have eaten. A tiny portion of food may make them feel they have to do hundreds of push-ups or jumping jacks to get rid of the calories they have eaten. Intense exercise can put a weakened heart under even more pressure. Boys with eating disorders often exercise excessively to lose weight or improve their muscle definition.

CHAPTER THREE

WHO SUFFERS AND WHY?

Like many women, Abby's mom was always on a diet, trying to lose a few pounds. She would buy low-calorie foods and always talked about "good" foods and "bad" foods. Abby's sister was on her college track team and watched her weight. Abby liked sports, but didn't make any of her school teams. As she entered puberty, Abby began to gain some weight, a natural part of adolescent development. Very sensibly, Abby didn't pay any attention to it, and kept exercising moderately and eating healthily. However, one day, an unkind remark about her body shape triggered a change in Abby's life that was to have a devastating effect. Abby began to diet. She became self-conscious about her body and weight, constantly looking at herself in the mirror. She believed she was fat and that this meant she was a failure. She skipped meals but was then so hungry that she binged on the foods she was trying to avoid.

UNDERCOVER STORY
DEADLY DIETING

Worryingly, a *Time* magazine report showed that 80 percent of children have been on a diet by the time they reach fourth grade. Dieting can trigger disordered eating, which can lead to serious eating disorders.

BREAKING NEWS

>> According to the National Institute of Mental Health (NIMH), boys and men are increasingly suffering from eating disorders.

DIETS THAT LEAD TO EATING DISORDERS

Experts believe that dieting is the most common cause of eating disorders. What may start as a reduction in calories to lose a few pounds can lead to an obsession with food and weight, and a serious eating disorder. Some people, like Abby's mother, are able to manage diets reasonably, without them leading to eating disorders. However, for Abby, dieting led to years of an eating disorder and severe physical and psychological harm.

Any one of these young people could suffer from an eating disorder.

The shame they often feel from being associated from what was considered a "girls' disease" makes them reluctant to ask for professional help.

Adolescents are particularly vulnerable to developing eating disorders. Teenagers have lots to cope with. Their bodies and minds are going through many changes as they mature into adulthood. A rush of hormones (chemicals in the body) put them on a roller-coaster ride of emotions.

USING FOOD TO COPE

There are many issues that affect young people, from problems at home to problems at school or with friends. Some young people can't cope with these issues and, instead of dealing with them, try to blot out their pain in disordered eating patterns. They are often unaware that they are using food as a way of coping. The painful truth is that an eating disorder doesn't get rid of other problems such as family breakup or bullying—it just adds to the unhappiness.

Some teenagers don't want to face the responsibilities and challenges of the adult world and don't feel ready for it. Girls often don't want their bodies to develop more grown-up curves and a more rounded shape—being underweight chains their body to childhood.

UNDERCOVER STORY

PUBERTY AND EATING DISORDERS

A research study by the National Institute of Mental Health indicated that physical changes, along with psychological changes, during puberty may be related to the development of bulimia and binge eating in young teenagers.

BREAKING NEWS

>> Statistics from the Alliance for Eating Disorders Awareness show that 90 percent of those who have eating disorders are women between the ages of 12 and 25. An estimated 11 percent of high

For some young people, food becomes a way of escaping from pressures, such as schoolwork, that they feel unable to cope with.

school students have been diagnosed with an eating disorder. Anorexia is the third most common chronic illness among adolescents. A chronic illness is one that is persistent and long-lasting.

27

Bullying takes many forms, including name-calling, unkind comments on social networking sites, and excluding someone from friendship groups. Bullying can be extremely destructive—it lowers self-esteem and makes a person feel isolated and frightened. Cruel teasing about weight is a form of bullying. The danger of this type of bullying is that it can trigger a person to embark on a very restrictive diet that quickly escalates into anorexia.

Deliberately leaving someone out and making unkind comments is a form of bullying and leads to low self-esteem. This can be the trigger for an eating disorder.

BREAKING NEWS

>> According to a survey carried out by the charity BEAT in 2012, out of 600 people questioned, 90 percent said they had been bullied. Seventy-eight percent of people with

BULLYING AND EATING DISORDERS
Teasing about weight and looks is a type of bullying. People may think the comments are harmless, but they can be devastating for the victim who turns the negative feelings toward their relationship with food. Of course, many people who experience bullying do not develop eating disorders, but for others it is the trigger that causes an agonizing and lonely disorder.

Any kind of bullying lowers victims' self-esteem and makes them feel worthless. Low self-esteem lies at the root of many eating disorders.

Whether it is verbal taunts, teasing, or physical aggression, bullying has long-lasting effects. By the time the bully has stopped, or moved on to another victim, the sufferer may be caught up in an eating disorder that spirals out of control.

UNDERCOVER STORY
DANGEROUS ADVICE
Some social networking and some web sites try to encourage people into a life of eating disorders and emotional and physical pain. The sites promote eating disorders, such as anorexia, calling them lifestyle choices. They taunt people on the sites to lose more and more weight. These so-called "pro ana" sites try to promote eating disorders as a lifestyle choice, but they ignore the physical and emotional harm caused by eating disorders.

eating disorders acknowledged that bullying had led to their disorder. Over 40 percent of respondents said they were under the age of 10 when the bullying started.

Adolescents face a lot of peer pressure and media pressure to behave and look a certain way. They begin to believe that having a slim body is all that matters to anyone. People with eating disorders often project all their hopes onto their body shape—they think that if they are thinner, they will be happier. They may be a healthy weight, but when they look in the mirror, they see someone who is fat. The dissatisfaction with body image continues the unhealthy cycle of dieting and bingeing.

ATHLETES AND EATING DISORDERS

Athletes and people who take part in activities such as dance and gymnastics are particularly vulnerable to developing eating disorders. A study of runners by the University of Leeds, England, in 2001 found that of 184 female athletes, 16 percent had an eating disorder. Today, coaches and teachers are trained to spot signs of possible problems and to offer support where needed.

Opposite: Eating disorders are common in activities where there is relentless pressure to maintain a particular shape and weight.

HITTING THE HEADLINES
PAINFUL SUCCESS

As a young competitive gymnast, Jennifer Sey was used to regular weigh-ins to check her weight. According to Jennifer's memoirs, coaches shouted at the gymnasts if they had gained any weight, saying it would affect their performance and ability. At the top of her profession, Sey was regularly bingeing and purging, desperate not to gain weight.

BREAKING NEWS

>> According to a 2010 American Viewpoint survey, 70 percent of people believe encouraging the media and advertisers to use more average-sized people in their advertising campaigns would reduce or prevent eating disorders.

CHAPTER FOUR

GETTING HELP

Janine was in her mid-twenties before she admitted she suffered from an eating disorder. Until then, she had just about managed to hold down a job but hardly had a social life. Instead, she was caught up in a destructive pattern of dieting, bingeing, and purging. Her weight was up and down. She had distanced herself from her family because she was trying to be independent. They also got mad at her when she wouldn't share family meals and enjoy the occasion. Janine didn't want to admit she had an eating disorder because she didn't want to face the issues that had caused her to find comfort in food.

It can take a long time before someone admits to having an eating disorder and seeks help to recover.

TURNING POINT

It got to the stage where Janine could see no point to her life anymore. She was desperate to eat normally and to be happy wearing shorts and T-shirts like other people, whatever their size and shape. Yet, no matter how many promises she made to herself that today would be different, Janine was unable to stop the painful wheel of dieting, bingeing, and purging on which she was caught.

Eventually, Janine broke down and confided in an old friend who knew someone else who had also suffered from an eating disorder. The friend reassured Janine that she could get better but that she needed help and support. Janine started to see a counselor. There was no magic cure, but the counselor helped Janine focus on ways to feel better about herself. Her eating pattern slowly began to improve.

UNDERCOVER STORY
ENOUGH SUPPORT?

According to the American Academy of Child and Adolescent Psychiatry, "With comprehensive treatment, most teenagers can be relieved of the symptoms or helped to control eating disorders." However, a study by the National Institute of Mental Health reports that even though 3 percent of American adolescents are affected by an eating disorder, most do not receive treatment for their specific eating condition.

People who suffer from eating disorders are often extremely secretive about their condition and go to great lengths to cover up their problem. As a result, the eating disorder may continue, unchecked by a medical professional, for a very long time. It is often not until family and friends finally recognize and point out that there is something wrong that a diagnosis takes place.

Sufferers are often reluctant to admit they have a problem with food, but research shows that the early treatment of eating disorders increases the speed and likelihood of recovery. The longer a person is caught in the grip of an eating disorder, the harder it can be for them to break free. This is why it is so important for people to recognize the key signs of an eating disorder in family or friends, or even themselves.

An unhealthy focus on body weight and image is just one possible sign of bulimia.

SIGNS OF EATING DISORDERS

The signs that a person may have, or may be developing, an eating disorder include:

- low self-esteem, constantly putting himself or herself down
- constantly referring to weight or body shape
- avoiding meals and making excuses about not eating
- becoming very particular about order and tidiness, getting upset if things are not in the correct place
- spending a lot of time in the bathroom
- wearing baggy clothes in an attempt to disguise weight loss

If a person displays some of these signs it may be an indication that he or she has an eating disorder. By understanding and recognizing the signs, family members and friends of a sufferer may be able to intervene and encourage the person to seek help.

UNDERCOVER STORY

IS IT IN THE GENES?

Scientists are researching possible biological causes of eating disorders. In some individuals with eating disorders, certain chemicals in the brain that control hunger, appetite, and digestion have been found to be unbalanced. Eating disorders often run in families and current research suggests that there may be a genetic link.

BREAKING NEWS

>> According to statistics from the South Carolina Department of Mental Health, treatment of an eating disorder in the United States ranges from $500 per day to $2,000 per day.

There is no quick fix for an eating disorder. Some people think sufferers just need to eat regular, reasonable meals to "cure" themselves. However, that is incredibly hard for someone with an eating disorder to do. A person with an eating disorder has a locked and distorted way of thinking about food. It takes specialized support to unlock it so the sufferer can learn how to eat for health again.

Recovery takes time and involves addressing both an individual's physical and emotional needs. People have to find new ways of dealing with the stresses and challenges of their lives, without using food as a coping mechanism.

Recovery from an eating disorder can take a long time because sufferers have to face the emotional issues that they were previously blocking out with their disordered use of food.

ROAD TO RECOVERY

The first step to recovery is admitting that there is a problem. Some people receive inpatient treatment either in a hospital or in a center that specializes in eating disorders. Their food intake is closely monitored to make sure their bodies are recovering. Counseling encourages sufferers to talk about their feelings and find ways to deal with their problems. Family therapy often helps sufferers and their families deal with issues or problems that contributed to the eating disorder. One of the most difficult decisions to make when a person is life-threateningly underweight is whether or not to force-feed them. Parents or carers of young people are usually allowed to make that difficult decision, but the issue is more complex when doctors are treating adults. People with anorexia often don't even want a drip put into their body to rehydrate them because they fear that the fluid will make them gain weight.

UNDERCOVER STORY
IS IT ALL IN THE BRAIN?

One study by Columbia University showed that women with bulimia had different brain activity patterns from those of women who did not have an eating disorder. Increased research into the causes and nature of eating disorders will help health professionals provide improved treatment for sufferers. People with anorexia may be helped to recover with a type of pacemaker that is inserted under the skin. The device sends electrical impulses to an area of the brain linked to appetite and mood. A study in Canada showed an improvement in the condition of the patients who were treated with the pacemaker.

CHAPTER FIVE

THE IMPORTANCE OF WELL-BEING

Beyond Stereotypes is a study commissioned by Dove in 2005. The study surveyed 3,300 girls and women between the ages of 15 and 64 in 10 countries and discovered that 67 percent of all women in this age group stopped certain activities because they felt unhappy about their looks.

In 2011, Condé Nast, international publisher of *Vogue* and other magazines, declared that its editors would not use models who were so thin they looked like they had eating disorders. Many people believe that the use of such thin models adds to young people's feelings of dissatisfaction with their own bodies, and the pressure to be size zero, and starts the cycle of dieting that so often leads to disordered eating patterns.

The use of ultrathin models puts pressure on girls and boys to look a certain way.

BREAKING NEWS

>> According to a study published in *Nutrition Today*, 69 percent of American elementary school girls who read magazines say that the pictures influence their concept of the ideal body shape. Forty-seven percent say the pictures make them want to lose weight.

THE IDEAL BODY

Western society presents an image of a so-called ideal body that is far from the reality of most people. Clothes are designed for and modeled by thin shapes. The body type portrayed in advertising as the ideal is possessed naturally by only 5 percent of American females, according to the Renfrew Center Foundation for Eating Disorders.

Eating disorders often stem from low self-esteem, feeling not good enough or worthless. Taking control over food (or losing control over it) is used to dull the unhappiness that the person feels. However an eating disorder only buries the cause of the unhappiness—it doesn't solve it. The media has an important role in helping boys and girls focus on their qualities and strengths as people, rather than their weight and body image.

Media images of muscular men can make boys feel dissatisfied with their bodies.

People with eating disorders find it extremely difficult to judge clearly what is a reasonable amount of food for a healthy body. They no longer recognize what normal eating is. It takes time and patience for them to recover a sense of perspective. They need support to accept and understand that the body needs a balance of carbohydrates, fats, protein, and vitamins. A reasonable amount of exercise also keeps a person fit and healthy. People with eating disorders need to relearn how to eat for health and well-being.

ON THE RISE

Eating disorders are on the rise, but so is childhood obesity, which stems from unhealthy diets and not enough exercise. Programs to reduce obesity and promote healthy eating are extremely important because obesity puts young people at a greater risk of developing many serious illnesses such as diabetes and heart disease. It is also important not to create anxiety and worry among children about their body shape and image, which can then lead to a cycle of harmful eating disorders.

HITTING THE HEADLINES
FIGHTING CHILDHOOD OBESITY

Let's Move is Michelle Obama's initiative to combat childhood obesity. Obama's program is in response to the growing obesity problem in the United States, with one in three children overweight or obese. This is partly due to the changing eating patterns that have developed in modern times. These include more snacking, larger portion sizes, more fat and sugars in processed foods, and a more sedentary lifestyle as children spend a greater amount of time on computers and gaming devices. *Let's Move* is designed to encourage a positive attitude to healthy eating and exercise.

A RESPONSIBILITY

Society has a responsibility to ensure that young people understand that healthy eating is about balanced, nutritious meals, and not about a spiral of diets.

Michelle Obama is a leading figure in the campaign to get young people fit and healthy with a balanced and positive attitude to food and eating.

Positive self-esteem helps prevent eating disorders and supports a person's recovery. Recovery from eating disorders is about learning to accept oneself and to nourish the body. Avoiding diets helps a person concentrate on healthy eating rather than trying to become thin or cut out complete food groups. Nutritionists can give sufferers specific advice and support about how to create a healthy and well-balanced diet.

The road to recovery from an eating disorder is a long one, with ups and downs. It's important to support individuals and help them to realize that while there may be setbacks and disappointments in their recovery, it doesn't mean that they have failed.

Opposite: Many high-profile figures such as Demi Lovato are now involved in campaigns to raise young people's self-esteem and confidence about their bodies.

HITTING THE HEADLINES

RAISING SELF-ESTEEM

Disney star Demi Lovato battled with anorexia and bulimia for many years. Aware of the pressure she had felt to look a certain way, the singer teamed up with other celebrities and the Jed Foundation to promote a campaign called *Love Is Louder than the Pressure to be Perfect*. This is aimed particularly at teenage and college-age girls to improve their self-esteem and recognize their qualities and strengths.

DIFFERENT BODIES

Everyone is different and unique and has special qualities to offer and share. There is no perfect person or perfect body shape. Everyone has flaws and it's important for people to learn to accept their flaws, without judging themselves too harshly.

It's also useful to challenge media presentations of girls and women, as well as boys and men. NEDA research suggests that the public sees over 3,000 commercials each day containing messages that encourage girls and women to feel unhappy with their bodies.

EATING DISORDERS—THE TRUTH

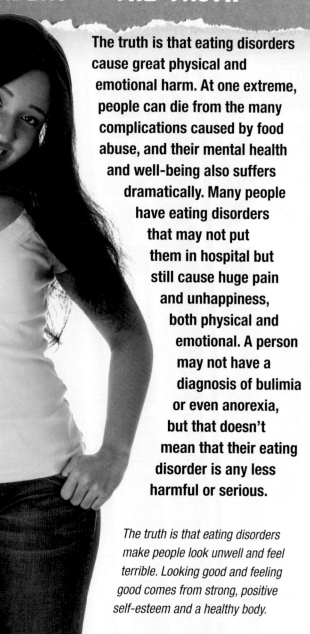

The truth is that eating disorders cause great physical and emotional harm. At one extreme, people can die from the many complications caused by food abuse, and their mental health and well-being also suffers dramatically. Many people have eating disorders that may not put them in hospital but still cause huge pain and unhappiness, both physical and emotional. A person may not have a diagnosis of bulimia or even anorexia, but that doesn't mean that their eating disorder is any less harmful or serious.

The truth is that eating disorders make people look unwell and feel terrible. Looking good and feeling good comes from strong, positive self-esteem and a healthy body.

STOPPING SUFFERING

Raising awareness of the dangers of eating disorders and ways in which to spot the signs of an eating disorder is crucial in the path to preventing these debilitating conditions. By recognizing and stopping an eating disorder in its early stages, individuals and their families could be saved years of physical and mental suffering.

As more research into eating disorders and their effects is carried out by the health industry, health professionals will be better able to understand the causes and triggers of these conditions. This research will then help sufferers receive the support they need to be able to deal with their problems and recover from their illnesses.

HITTING THE HEADLINES

THE ROAD TO RECOVERY

Today, 30-year-old Victor Avon from New Jersey is a healthy, successful spokesman for NEDA. However, for many years he suffered the agonies of anorexia. His story is not uncommon. Bullied at school for being overweight, Avon began to hate food and blamed it for all his problems. He stopped eating properly and for six years hid his anorexia. Eventually, he sought treatment and made a recovery. If people are informed about eating disorders, they will be better able to find help and support, and start on the long road to recovery.

GLOSSARY

addiction A condition in which the body and mind crave and depend on particular substances, such as food, drugs, or alcohol.

anorexia nervosa An eating disorder characterized by a person deliberately restricting his or her food intake and becoming very underweight.

binge To rapidly consume a large amount of food in a short amount of time.

bulimia An eating disorder with a bingeing and purging cycle.

carbohydrates A group of nutrients found in foods such as bread, pasta, rice, and starchy vegetables such as potatoes.

compulsive Unable to stop doing something.

diagnosis Identification of an illness or disorder by a health professional.

dehydration An abnormal loss of water from the body.

genetic Having to do with genes, the basic units of heredity.

media Television, newspapers, and the Internet.

mineral An element in food that the body needs for healthy growth and development.

nutrients Elements in food that provide the body with energy.

psychological Having to do with the mind.

peer Someone of a similar age.

puberty The physical and emotional changes that occur as older children develop into young adults.

purge To get rid of food by vomiting or taking laxatives in order to go to the bathroom.

obsession A state in which someone thinks about something all the time.

rational Reasoned; not illogical.

self-esteem Pride in or respect for oneself.

vitamins Substances found in foods that are essential for the normal and healthy working of the body.

FOR MORE INFORMATION

BOOKS

Allman, Tony. *Eating Disorders*. San Diego, CA: Lucent Books, 2010.

Gillard, Arthur. *Eating Disorders*. Farmington Hills, MI: Greenhaven Press, 2010.

Parks, Peggy J. *Teenage Eating Disorders: Compact Research*. San Diego, CA: Reference Point Press, 2011.

Warbrick, Caroline. *Eating Disorders and Body Image*. London, UK: Wayland, 2012.

ORGANIZATIONS

Teen Line
P.O. Box 48750
Los Angeles, CA 90048
(310) 855-HOPE (4673) or (800)
TLC-TEEN (852-8336)
Web site: http://teenlineonline.org
A site and phone line run for teens by teens that deals with a variety of issues that affect young people.

WEB SITES

Due to the changing nature of Internet links, Rosen Publishing has developed an online list of Web sites related to the subject of this book. This site is updated regularly. Please use this link to access the list:

http://www.rosenlinks.com/UCS/Eat

INDEX

advertising images 30,
38, 39, 43
anorexia 6–9, 16–17,
21, 22, 27, 28, 37, 45
athletes 30

binge eating 7, 10, 11, 12,
13, 15, 20, 22, 26, 30
biological causes 35
body image 4, 8, 24, 30,
38, 39, 40
boys and men 5, 7, 23,
24, 39, 45
brain activity 37
bulimia 7, 10–11, 15,
18, 19, 21, 22, 26, 37
bullying 26, 28–29, 45

celebrity sufferers
18–19, 21, 42
compulsive eating
disorders 12, 13
constipation 18
coping mechanism, food
as 12, 20, 26, 27, 36, 39
counseling 33, 37
cycle of behavior 11, 15,
20, 30, 32, 33, 40

death 8, 9, 14, 15, 16
dehydration 7, 18
diabetes 13, 40
diarrhea 18
diets 4, 9, 11, 12, 24, 25,
28, 38, 42

EDNOS (Eating Disorders
Not Otherwise
Specified) 13
exercise 6, 22, 23, 40

faintness and dizziness
16, 18
families and friends
22, 37
family therapy 37
fear of food 4, 9
force-feeding 37

genetic links 35

hair, downy 16
hair loss 6, 16
heart problems 7, 13,
16, 18, 23, 40
hospitalization 6, 10, 37

John, Elton 21

Lady Gaga 21
laxatives 10, 18
Lovato, Demi 42

mental illness 8, 15
models 9, 38

Obama, Michelle 40, 41
obesity 40
obsession with food 6, 25
esophagus, damaged 18
osteoporosis 17
overweight 12, 13

periods 17
potassium 18
"pro ana" web sites 29
puberty 24, 26
purging 10, 11, 20, 30

recovery 5, 21, 34,
36–37, 40, 42

Scherzinger, Nicole 19
secrecy 9, 10, 11, 21,
22, 34
self-esteem, low 28, 29,
35, 39
self-loathing 11, 19
shame 11, 13, 15, 20, 25
signs of eating
disorders 34, 35
socializing, avoidance of
13, 22, 23
sores and blisters 18
sour breath 6
stunted growth 18
suicide 14, 16

teasing 29
teenagers 5, 18, 26, 33
tooth decay 18
treatment costs 35
triggers 28, 29

unhappiness 11, 13, 17,
20, 22, 26, 39

vomiting 10, 18

weight, checking 6, 30